God cares when I'm Sad

by Denise Vezey
Illustrated by Victoria Ponikvar Frazier

A Faith Parenting Guide
can be found on page 32

Dedicated to

Our daughter, Brynne, who inspired me to write this book.

Proverbs 17:22

Faith Kids is an imprint of
Cook Communications, Colorado Springs, Colorado 80918
Cook Communications, Paris, Ontario
Kingsway Communications, Eastbourne, England

GOD CARES WHEN I AM SAD
© 2000 by Denise Vezey for text and Victoria Ponikvar Frazier for illustrations.

Edited by Jeannie Harmon
Designed by Sonya Design and Illustration

First printing, 2000
Printed in Canada
04 03 02 01 00   5 4 3 2 1

Library of Congress Cataloging-in-Publication Data

Vezey, Denise.
        God cares when I'm sad / by Denise Vezey; illustrated by Victoria Ponikvar Frazier.
                p. cm. (Getting to Know God series)
                Summary: Although she is sad when her balloon pops, when her
        expected new baby sister turns out to be a boy, and when rain
        threatens to ruin her family picnic, a girl realizes that God cares
        when she is not happy.
                ISBN 0-7814-3070-4
                [1. Sadness Fiction. 2. Christian life Fiction.] I. Frazier, Victoria
        Ponikvar, 1966-   ill. II. Title. III. Series.
        PZ7.V627Gn 2000
        [E]--dc21

                                                                                    99-17033
                                                                                         CIP

Table of Contents

My balloon broke

A birthday, a party,
I am going to a birthday party!
My best friend is turning six,
and everyone will get a balloon!
I can hardly wait!

I clap, I laugh, I giggle.
I skip, I hop, I wiggle.

I put on my dress
and sing songs in my room.
Joyful and happy,
I'll get a balloon!

I go to Casey's house in my party dress.
All my friends are there.
We play pin-the-nose-on-the-clown
and eat yummy cake.

Casey gives each of us a balloon.

My balloon is purple and shiny.

It's as big as the moon
and floats high above me.
I love it!
I can't wait to show my daddy.

"Daddy, oh Daddy,
see what I got at the party?
See my pretty" . . . POP!

My pretty purple balloon is gone!
One minute it was here
and the next . . . BANG!
I feel so sad.

"Come here, Dumpling," says Daddy.

Daddy gently says,
"God knows it makes us sad
to lose something we like.
But He promises to hold us
just like I'm holding you."

Daddy says, "Would this make you feel better."

He pulls a surprise out of his pocket.

It's a pretty pink balloon.

He takes a deep breath and blows it up for me.

I clap, I laugh, I wiggle.
I skip, I hop, I giggle.

When my balloon broke,
God knew I was sad.
I know that He cares
and now I am glad.

My baby is a boy

Guess what?
I'm getting a little sister!
I help Mommy get ready.
I fold nightgowns and clean toys.
Mommy is having a baby!

I whistle, I wash, I wait.
I sweep, I mark the date.

A new little life
will bring us such joy.
But I wish and I hope
she won't be a boy!

I talk to our baby in Mommy's tummy.
I say, "Hi, little baby. I can't wait to see you.
Are you cozy and warm in there?"

When she comes home, she will know my voice.

The big day is here!

Daddy takes Mommy to the hospital.

I stay with Grandma.

We wait by the phone.

Ring-a-ling-a-ling . . .

It's Daddy!

"Mommy and the baby are fine.
Do you want to know the baby's name?"
"Yes, Daddy, yes. Tell me!"
Daddy says, "Scott."
The baby's name is Scott!

"How can you name a girl Scott?" I ask.

"He's not a girl, honey. Mommy had a baby boy."

"Oh." I am very quiet.

Boys aren't bad, but I wanted a girl.

In a few days,
Mommy comes home with the baby.
I put my finger in his hand,
and he grabs it very hard!
He will not let go!
My baby brother is very strong.

Daddy asks, "Are you sad your baby isn't a girl?"
I shake my head yes.

"Even though the baby
isn't the little girl you wanted,
God knew we needed a little boy to love."

I rock him, I hold him, he burps!
I change him, I find him a shirt.

A new little life
has brought us such joy.
Now I am so glad
my baby is a boy.

My picnic washed away

I made up a song.
Would you like to hear it?
We're going on a picnic by the blue, blue sea.
We're going on a picnic just my family and me.

I talk, I dream, I write.
I hope the sun is bright.

I pray it won't rain
on our special day.
"God, please don't let
my picnic wash away."

I wait and wait
for two whole weeks.
It's almost like waiting for Christmas!
Finally, it's the night before our picnic.

I lay awake and think.

It's just got to be warm

when we go to the shore.

How can I sleep?

I toss and turn. I'm tangled in my sheets!

It's morning. Oh-no!

What do I hear?

Pitter-patter. Pitter-patter. Pitter-patter.

Raindrops are falling everywhere.

The whole world is raining!

"Mommy, Mommy.
How can this be?
I prayed that it wouldn't rain,
but look out the window."

Our day at the beach is gone!

Mommy told me God sees every tear.
He cares when we are sad.
God loves us so much that He wants us
to tell Him all about our sad times.

What's all the noise downstairs?
Daddy says, "Put your swimming suit on,
grab your towel, and come down *quickly!*"
I do as he says.

What do I see?
A make-believe beach is waiting for me!

I swim, I dig, I play,
I eat, I sing all day.

I know that it rained
on our special day.
But I'm happy our picnic
did not wash away.

Dear God, I know that You see me when
I'm sad, and You understand how I feel.
Thank You for loving me!

Cast all your cares on him because he cares for you.
1 Peter 5:7 NIV

Faith Parenting Guide

God Cares When I'm Sad

Age: 4-7

Life Issue: My child needs to realize that God is there to help and comfort in times of disappointment.

Spiritual Building Block: Trust

Learning Styles

Sight: View a story video or a read story from a Bible story picture book that recounts times when people had to rely on God. Some examples are Daniel in the Lion's den, Queen Esther, Elijah and the prophets of Baal, and Jonah. How did these people know that they could trust God? How do we know that we can trust God?

Sound: When you hear an emergency vehicle siren, discuss with your child the different vehicles that use a siren. It usually means that help is on the way to someone in need. How do we know this? Can we believe that when we have a fire or are in an accident, someone will come and help us? Why?

Touch: Discuss with your child times that you were sad and how you trusted God to bring an answer to your situation. How were you comforted by knowing that God had everything under control? Ask your child to think of a person who is currently going through a sad time. Decide together what you can do to help that person feel God's comfort through your actions. Memorize I Peter 5:7 together and share it with that person.